No MSG For Me

COOKBOOK

If you have a MSG sensitivity, this is the cookbook for you. No MSG For Me is a collection of over 100 MSG free recipes.

Lisa Kramer

Printed in the United States of America

020409

ISBN: 978-0-615-25757-0

Library of Congress Control Number: 2008909684

Additional copies may be purchased at www.nomsgforme.com.

Thank You Notes

The whole idea of a cookbook came from Mike, my husband. He has faithfully tasted all my creations and shared in my excitement when we rediscovered a forbidden meal. With his encouragement, cooking has become empowering for me. No longer am I unable to enjoy my favorite meals. A big thank you to Mike for his unending love and support.

Many thanks to my mom who always welcomed my help in the kitchen as a child. My mom would take the Olympic gold medal for the record number of new recipes she tries. Dad always jokes that if we like the new meal we will never have it again because mom will be too busy trying something new. We love you mom. A big thank you to my mom who gave me the creativity to try new things and for my love of good eats.

Lastly, thanks to God for always providing our daily bread. I am truly blessed!

Table of Contents

Introduction

Since you are looking at this cookbook, it is likely that you or someone you know has a monosodium glutamate (MSG) sensitivity. Or maybe, you have made a decision to eliminate MSG from your diet for general health reasons.

For me it all came to light back in 2004. I was 27 years old and normally a very energetic woman who enjoyed a variety of food. I found myself nauseous, tired and worn out. It didn't matter if I ate or not because I felt sick either way. Often when I did eat, my stomach rejected the food and within 20 minutes I was on the toilet. I know, it's not a pretty picture, but I'm sure some of you with a MSG sensitivity can relate.

After several trips to my doctor's office with no real improvement, my mother took things into her own hands. Thankfully, she dragged me to a natural health specialist where I was told that my body was sensitive to MSG. It was not the "ah-ha" moment I was hoping for, but it did give me some direction.

After Google-ing MSG and finding a million trillion hits, I realized that so many of my favorite foods had MSG. I had heard of MSG, but who knew about hydrolyzed protein and soy protein? I also learned that MSG reactions varied for each individual. In addition, a reaction could also differ depending on the amount of MSG and the frequency of exposures.

Keeping MSG off the table is no easy task. It took me 2 hours to complete my first grocery shopping trip. I left the store with only a quarter of the items on my list and was known as the "special diet" lady by the grocery clerks from that day forward. Would I ever be able to love food again?

No more Chinese food, chips or ranch dressing. Sausage, meatballs, fajitas and all those tasty casseroles made with cream of yummy soups. Seasoned fries, au jus dip, cocktail sauce and my father-in-law's mouth watering prime rib. All those foods that made me smack my lips and lick my fingers clean. All gone...

Determined that I would not lack good eats, I started experimenting. First, I found that higher quality brands often did not contain MSG. Quality brands consist of basic ingredients without preservatives and flavor enhancers. Natural products are often good options, but MSG is considered natural so be sure to read the label. Keep checking labels because many name brand products are beginning to eliminate MSG.

Second, I realized that when I make recipes from scratch I don't add MSG. I know it's easy to buy stuff right off the grocery store shelf, but I have found that homemade meals can be easy and tastier than the prepackaged.

Third, I just omit or substitute for soy sauce. You can add a small amount of salt instead or an alternative spice like ginger. Most of the time no one even notices the change.

Take note, I am by no means an expert on MSG sensitivity. I am a self taught person who has improved my daily living by avoiding MSG whenever possible.

So, here is a collection of recipes that have no MSG. Chances are that many of the recipes originally had MSG if you bought them at a restaurant or grocery store, but now you can make them at home MSG free. It is a cookbook that gives you a variety of recipes that are all MSG free.

Monosodium Glutamate

Monosodium glutamate (MSG) is used as a flavor enhancer in a variety of foods prepared at home, in restaurants and by food processors. It's an inexpensive way to make blah food taste better. Your taste buds love the sweet and salty sensation it provides. Its use has become controversial in the past 30 years because of reports of adverse reactions in people who have eaten foods that contain MSG.

Natural Glutamate vs. MSG

Here is a crash course on MSG…Natural glutamate can be found in food such as tomatoes, mushrooms and milk. The Glutamate Association at www.msgfacts.com states, "MSG's principal component is an amino acid called glutamic acid or glutamate. Glutamate is found naturally in protein-containing foods such as meat, vegetables, poultry and milk. The human body also produces glutamate naturally in large amounts. The muscles, brain and other body organs contain about four pounds of glutamate, and human milk is rich in glutamate, compared to cow's milk, for example.

Glutamate is found in two forms: "bound" glutamate (linked to other amino acids forming a protein molecule) and "free" glutamate (not linked to protein). Only free glutamate is effective in enhancing the flavor of food. "

Manufactured free glutamate is most often made from corn, molasses or wheat by a fermentation process. This substance is then mixed with salt and is known as monosodium glutamate or MSG. Then it's added to some food and presto, the flavor is improved.

This manufactured free glutamate or glutamic acid negatively affects those sensitive to MSG. At www.truthinlabeling.com it states, "manufactured free glutamic acid is found in processed foods, but it is not found in unprocessed or unadulterated meat, fish or vegetables (including soybeans, mushrooms, and tomatoes.). Only meat, fish or vegetables that have been subjected to some sort of manufacturing or fermenting process will cause MSG reactions in MSG sensitive people who ingest amounts that exceed their tolerances for MSG.

Dairy products, also, may cause MSG reactions in MSG sensitive people because some dairy products are ultra-pasteurized, some are fermented, and many contain food additives such as carrageenan that are problematic for MSG sensitive people. All manufactured free glutamic acid contains contaminants (D-glutamic acid, pyroglutamic acid, and others), while the glutamic acid found in intact/unadulterated protein contains no contaminants. "

So what does this all mean? Manufactured free glutamate is MSG and it's what MSG sensitive people react to most often. Keep in mind that everyone's tolerance level is different. You may find it helpful to keep a log of what ingredients work for you and what ones you should avoid in the future.

MSG Reactions

Common MSG reactions can include:

- Headache
- Flushing
- Sweating
- Sense of facial pressure or tightness
- Numbness, tingling or burning in or around the mouth
- Rapid, fluttering heartbeats (heart palpitations)

- Chest pain
- Shortness of breath
- Nausea
- Weakness
- Diarrhea

Citric Acid

Many MSG sensitive individuals also react to citric acid. Even if you can tolerate citrus fruits, you may be intolerant of citric acid because it is most likely made from corn. Its uses in processed food include flavoring, balancing of acid-alkalinity levels, as a preservative, as a firming agent and as an antibacterial agent.

Citric acid is produced by fermentation of crude sugars. When citric acid is produced from corn, manufacturers do not take the time or money to remove all corn protein. During processing, the remaining protein is hydrolyzed, resulting in some processed free glutamic acid (MSG). Citric acid may also interact with any protein in the food to which it is added, freeing up more glutamic acid.

For more information check out Debby Anglesey's Battling the "MSG Myth", A Survival Guide and Cookbook. It provides an in depth look at MSG.

Labeling & MSG

It is important to always carefully read the labels because ingredients constantly change. The ingredients listed in this book are, at the time of printing, all MSG free. However, ingredients in any type of product may change at any given time and could vary depending on the region it was produced in.

MSG is frequently hidden in foods since there are no strict labeling guidelines. Often MSG is a component of another ingredient and therefore not labeled as containing MSG.

Sources of MSG that contain the highest percentage of manufactured glutamate

- autolyzed protein
- autolyzed yeast
- calcium caseinate
- glutamate
- glutamic acid
- gelatin
- hydrolyzed corn gluten
- hydrolyzed protein
- hydrolyzed wheat extract
- monosodium glutamate (MSG)
- monopotassium glutamate
- natrium glutamate
- sodium caseinate
- textured vegetable protein
- vegetable protein extract
- yeast extract
- yeast food
- yeast nutrient

Sometimes Sources of MSG

- anything fermented
- anything protein fortified
- anything enzyme modified
- barley malt
- bouillon
- broth
- caramel flavoring
- carrageenan
- citric acid
- cornstarch, fructose (made from corn)
- corn syrup
- corn, wheat, rice or oat protein
- enzymes anything
- fermented protein food
- flavors
- flavoring
- flowing agents
- lipolyzed butter fat
- malted barley
- malt extract
- malt flavoring
- maltodextrin, dextrose, dextrates
- modified food starch
- natural beef flavoring
- natural chicken flavoring
- natural flavor
- natural flavoring
- natural pork flavoring
- pectin
- protease
- protease enzymes
- protein fortified anything
- rice syrup

- seasonings
- soy protein
- soy protein concentrate
- soy protein isolate
- soy sauce
- soy sauce extract
- stock
- ultra-pasteurized
- whey protein
- whey protein concentrate
- whey protein isolate

For more information check out www.truthinlabeling.org, www.msgfacts.com and www.msgmyths.com.

 ## MSG Free Ingredients

The ingredients listed below are used in the cookbook. I have included some products that I use. Review the list to ensure that your cupboards are free from MSG products. Use the checklist to eliminate any MSG that may be hidden in your kitchen.

Take note that that the ingredients in these recipes do not affect me, but depending on your level of sensitivity, some may trouble you.

- ☐ **Bacon** – look for all natural
- ☐ **Beef Broth** – *Swanson's All Natural Beef Broth*
- ☐ **BBQ Sauce** – check label for corn syrup and citric acid. I make my own.
- ☐ **Butter** – avoid those with annatto, citric acid and natural flavoring. *Kirkland Organic Butter*
- ☐ **Canned Tuna** – look for tuna and water only

- [ ] **Cereal** - *Nature's Path Organic Corn Flakes*
- [ ] **Chicken and Turkey** – look for no additives or preservatives. I use organic free range chicken.
- [ ] **Chicken Broth** – *Rachel Ray's Stock-In-A-Pot All Natural Chicken Broth*
- [ ] **Chips** – *Ruffles Plain Potato Chips*, organic tortilla chips
- [ ] **Flour** – *Gold Medal Organic White Flour*
- [ ] **Jam** – highly sensitive people may be affected by the pectin
- [ ] **Ketchup** – *Muir Glen Organic Ketchup, Trader Joe Organic Ketchup or Full Circle Organic Ketchup*
- [ ] **Milk** – Organic whole milk is often a good choice.
- [ ] **Mustard** – dry mustard or organic prepared mustards
- [ ] **Nuts** – buy plain unseasoned quality nuts
- [ ] **Ranch Seasoning** – *Uncle Dan's Classic Ranch Seasoning Mix*
- [ ] **Oil** - use sunflower oil, extra-virgin olive oil or butter
- [ ] **Olive Oil** – organic, all natural extra-virgin olive oil
- [ ] **Parmesan Cheese** – Parmesan cheese is rich in natural occurring glutamate. Imported cheese is better. Some people tolerate it better than others.
- [ ] **Peanut Butter** – organic or all natural are better. *All Natural Laura Scudder's Old Fashion Peanut Butte*r
- [ ] **Pickles** - *Farman's Pickles*
- [ ] **Popcorn** – dry natural kernels
- [ ] **Pork, Sausage and Ham** – all natural and no additives. I have the luxury have having a whole pig butchered for me and I ensure nothing is added.
- [ ] **Processed Meats** – all natural and no additives
- [ ] **Salsa** - look for all natural ones that don't contain citric acid
- [ ] **Salt** – kosher, canning salt and some sea salts
- [ ] **Seasoning Blend for Steak** - *Montreal Steak Seasoning* by McCormick or a little salt and pepper
- [ ] **Sour Cream** – look for products without carrageenan and additives

- ☐ **Spaghetti Sauce** – look for products without citric acid and corn syrup
- ☐ **Sugar** – white cane sugar. *Organic & Fair Trade Sugar*. Brown sugar can contain molasses, which some people react to.
- ☐ **Taco Seasonings** – *McCormick No MSG Added Taco Seasoning*, but it has citric acid or if you want to avoid citric acid make your own from page 131.
- ☐ **Tomato Paste** – *Contadina Tomato Paste* or *Muir Glen Organic Tomato Paste*
- ☐ **Tomato Sauce** – look for no citric acid. *Muir Glen Organic Tomato Sauce* has naturally derived citric acid.
- ☐ **Tortillas** – avoid those with L-systeine
- ☐ **Whipping Cream** – look for products without carrageenan or additives
- ☐ **Yogurt** – plain whole milk yogurt is best. Try to avoid those that contain carrageenan, corn syrup, gelatin, pectin, gums, natural flavors, milk solids and lowfat.

You will also find another reminder within the recipes. Ingredients followed by a ✔ could contain MSG. Check the label if you have not already ensured that it does not contain MSG.

REFERENCES

Debbie Anglesey, *Battling the "MSG Myth"* (Front Porch Productions, 2007)

www.truthinlabeling.org

www.msgfacts.com

Appetizers

Bacon & Swiss

This quick and easy spread will make any vegetable taste good.

8 bacon slices ✔
8 oz. softened cream cheese
½ cup mayonnaise
2 teaspoons Dijon mustard ✔
1 ½ cups shredded Swiss cheese
3 chopped scallions
½ cup chopped almonds
Selection for dipping - baby carrots, celery, sliced baguettes, pumpernickel or rye bread

1. Preheat oven to 400 degrees F.
2. Brown bacon over medium heat. Drain bacon on paper towels and chop into bacon bits.
3. In a mixing bowl, combine bacon, cream cheese, mayonnaise, mustard, cheese and scallions. Place in a 2-quart baking dish. Bake for 15 minutes or until golden.
4. Top with almonds and serve with carrots, celery and breads.

BBQ Quesadillas

An appetizer that's filling as well as tasty. It's great for a party or even for lunch when paired with a green salad.

8 – 6 inch flour tortillas ✔
3 chicken breasts, cooked and thinly sliced ✔
½ cup BBQ sauce ✔
1 cup chopped red pepper
¼ cup chopped onion
1 cup shredded Cheddar and Monterey Jack cheese
Oil ✔

1. Preheat oven to 425 degrees F.
2. In a medium mixing bowl, mix chicken and BBQ sauce.
3. Place 4 tortillas on large cookie sheet or stoneware. Divide chicken evenly over 4 tortillas. Top each with equal amounts of red pepper, onion and cheese. Top each with a second tortilla.
4. Lightly spray the top of each tortilla with oil.
5. Bake for 10 minutes or until tops are lightly browned.
6. Cool for 5 minutes.
7. Cut into wedges with a scissors or pizza cutter.

Buffalo Wings

This chicken is both moist and flavorful. Try dipping it in the Blue Cheese Sauce or the Ranch Dressing.

12 whole chicken wings ✔
½ cup butter ✔
1 small clove garlic, minced
¼ cup hot sauce
½ teaspoon kosher salt
Celery sticks
Blue Cheese Dipping Sauce (recipe found on page 111) or Ranch
  Dressing (recipe found on page 128)

1. Place a 6-quart saucepan with a steamer basket and 1 inch of water in the bottom, over high heat, cover and bring to a boil.
2. Remove the tips of the wings and discard. Using kitchen shears, or a knife, separate the wings at the joint. Place the wings into the steamer basket, cover, reduce the heat to medium and steam for 10 minutes. Remove the wings from the basket and carefully pat dry. Lay the wings out on a cooling rack set in a half sheet pan lined with paper towels and place in the refrigerator for 1 hour.
3. Preheat the oven to 425 degrees F.
4. Replace the paper towels with parchment paper. Roast on the middle rack of the oven for 20 minutes. Turn the wings over and cook another 20 minutes or until meat is cooked through and the skin is golden brown.
5. While the chicken is roasting, melt the butter in a small bowl along with the garlic. Pour this along with hot sauce and salt into a bowl large enough to hold all of the chicken and stir to combine.

6. Remove the wings from the oven, transfer to the bowl and toss with the sauce. Serve warm along with celery sticks and blue cheese dipping sauce.

Creamy Red Pepper Dip

1 7oz. jar sweet roasted red peppers, drained and chopped
1 garlic clove, minced
1 tablespoon basil leaves
1 cup sour cream ✔
1 cup mayonnaise
½ teaspoon salt ✔
1 red pepper
8 cups assorted vegetables - carrots, celery, cucumber, broccoli, cauliflower, pea pods, zucchini or mushrooms

1. In a medium mixing bowl, add roasted peppers, garlic, basil, sour cream, mayonnaise and salt. Mix well.
2. Cut red pepper in half. Remove membranes and seeds. Fill red pepper with dip.
3. Serve with assorted vegetables.

Deviled Eggs

Don't forget this popular appetizer when planning a party. It is making a comeback at many special occasions. I can always count on my sister, Amy, to bring these to a party. The simple ingredients can usually be found right in your refrigerator.

6 hard cooked eggs, peeled
3 tablespoons mayonnaise
½ teaspoon dry mustard
1/8 teaspoon salt ✓
¼ teaspoon pepper
Paprika

Cut eggs lengthwise in half. Remove egg yolks and mash them with a fork. Add mayonnaise, mustard, salt and pepper. Fill egg whites with egg yolk mixture and dust the tops lightly with paprika.

Step It Up a Notch...You can add a dash of hot sauce, 1 teaspoon of chopped tarragon leaves and/or 1 tablespoon chopped chives to the egg yolk mixture.

Quesadillas

¾ cup chutney (recipes found on page 108, 118 & 126)
12 – 6 inch flour tortillas
1 ½ cups grated Cheddar cheese
¾ cup sour cream ✔
Salsa ✔

1. Preheat grill.
2. Spread 2 tablespoons of chutney over each of the 6 tortillas. Sprinkle ¼ cup of cheese over chutney. Top with remaining 6 tortillas. Grill until cheese is melted and the tortillas are golden. About 2 minutes per side.
3. Using a sharp knife or scissors, cut each tortilla into 6 wedges. Serve with sour cream and salsa.

Stuffed Mushrooms

This is a melt in your mouth recipe from my sister, Wendi, which is always a hit at the party.

50 large mushrooms
1 cup mayonnaise
3 oz. Parmesan cheese ✔
1 cup grated jack cheese
1 lb. bacon, cooked and crumbled ✔

1. Preheat oven to 350 degrees F.
2. Wash and remove stems from mushrooms. Set aside.
3. Combine mayonnaise, cheese and bacon. Spoon into mushroom caps. Do not overfill.
4. Bake for 20 minutes or until cheese is slightly golden.

Tortilla Pinwheels

This was one of my 4-H food demonstrations that won a blue ribbon at the Northwest Washington Fair in Lynden, Washington. Go green!

8 oz. sour cream ✔
8 oz. cream cheese, softened
1 4oz. can black olives, drained
1 4oz. can green diced chilies, drained
1 cup shredded Cheddar cheese
½ cup diced green onions
½ teaspoon minced garlic
¼ teaspoon salt
6 - 8 inch four tortillas ✔

1. Mix sour cream, cream cheese, olives, chilies, cheese, green onions, garlic and salt together in a medium bowl. Divide the filling between the tortillas. Spread filling over the tortillas and roll up.
2. Cover tightly with plastic wrap. Refrigerate for at least 4 hours to allow the flavors to blend.
3. To serve, cut each roll into 6 slices with a serrated knife.

Turkey Tortilla Pinwheels

These festive pinwheels can be served as appetizers or left whole as a sandwich.

6 – 8 inch flour tortillas ✔
8 oz. softened cream cheese
6 tablespoons pecans, finely chopped
12 large lettuce leaves
¾ lb. thinly sliced deli turkey
1 16oz. can whole cranberry sauce
¼ cup chopped celery
2 green onions, thinly sliced

1. To assemble each tortilla roll, place tortilla on a piece of wax paper. Top each tortilla with 1/6 of cream cheese and spread within ¼ inch of the edge. Sprinkle with pecans. Top with 1 lettuce leaf, pressing lightly into cream cheese. Place 2 slices of turkey over the lettuce. Spread 2 tablespoons of cranberry sauce.
2. Roll up tortilla tightly. Repeat with remaining ingredients.
3. To serve, cut each roll into 6 slices with a serrated knife. Place on a lettuce lined platter.
4. Combine remaining cranberry sauce, celery and green onions. Place in a dish in the middle of the platter.

Main Dishes

Beef

BBQ Beef & Rice

2 lbs. stew meat
2 teaspoons oil ✔
1 10½ oz. can tomato soup
½ cup ketchup ✔
1/3 cup plain rice vinegar
1 teaspoon dry mustard
1 teaspoon paprika
1 teaspoon chili powder
2 teaspoons celery seed
2 tablespoons brown sugar ✔
2 teaspoons salt ✔
3 cups rice

1. Cut meat into 1 inch cubes. Brown meat in a large skillet with 2 teaspoons of oil. Add tomato soup, ketchup, vinegar, mustard, paprika, chili powder, celery seed, brown sugar and salt. Mix well. Cover and simmer for 2 hours or until meat is tender.
2. Cook rice according to directions. Serve meat mixture over rice.

Beef Kabobs

The thrill of the grill! A fresh marinade adds flavor to beef sirloin and is served with grilled vegetables.

2 lbs. boneless beef sirloin
3 cloves garlic, minced
2 teaspoons paprika
½ teaspoon ground turmeric
½ teaspoon ground cumin
1 teaspoon salt ✔
½ teaspoon pepper
1/3 cup plain rice vinegar
½ cup extra-virgin olive oil ✔
1 red pepper
1 large onion
8 wooden skewers

1. Place skewers in water and allow to soak for at least 4 hours. Cut beef into 1 ½ inch cubes and place in a self seal bag. Set aside. In the bowl of a food processor combine garlic, paprika, turmeric, cumin, salt, pepper and vinegar. With the food processor running, drizzle in the olive oil. Pour marinade over meat and toss to coat. Place in the refrigerator and allow meat to marinade for 2 to 4 hours.
2. Cut onion and red pepper into 1 ½ inch cubes.
3. Preheat grill to medium-high heat.
4. Thread meat onto skewers leaving ½ inch between pieces. Repeat for onions and peppers. Brush onions and peppers with olive oil and salt. Place skewers on grill and cook with lid lowered. Cook 2 to 3 minutes per side; 8 to 12 minutes in all. Remove skewers from heat and place in aluminum foil. Wrap and allow skewers to rest for 3 minutes.

Curried Beef Pitas

This is an old favorite from my Aunt Louise. It has a rich flavor which can be adjusted to anyone's curry taste. Instead of the yogurt you can try some chutney which can be found on page 108, 118 and 126.

1 lb. ground beef
½ cup chopped onion
1 medium apple, peeled and chopped
¼ cup raisins
1 ¼ teaspoons salt ✔
1 teaspoon curry powder
1 8oz. plain yogurt, preferably Greek or sour cream ✔
4 pita breads, cut in half

1. In a large skillet over medium heat, cook ground beef, onion, apple, raisins, salt and curry.
2. When meat is fully cooked, spoon into pitas. Add a dollop of yogurt to each pita.

French Dip

Take pleasure as well as comfort in this savory dipped sandwich.

2 tablespoons butter ✔
1 shallot, chopped
1 tablespoon flour ✔
4 cups beef broth ✔
1 ½ pounds deli sliced roast beef
Seasoning blend for steak (I recommend Montreal Seasoning by McCormick)
4 sandwich rolls, split

1. In a large, shallow skillet over moderate heat, melt butter. Add shallots to butter and sauté 2 minutes. Add flour and cook 1 minute longer. Whisk in broth in a slow stream. Bring sauce to a boil and simmer over low heat until ready to serve the sandwiches.

2. Pile meat loosely across your cutting board. Season meat with grill seasoning or salt and pepper. Set out 4 small soup cups for dipping sauce, 4 dinner plates and 4 split rolls. To assemble, using a pair of kitchen tongs, dip meat into au jus sauce and pile into rolls. Set cups with extra dipping sauce along side the sandwiches.

Hamburger Cornbread Casserole

A casserole with a Tex-Mex flare is a great one dish meal. Serve with a dollop of sour cream.

1 lb. ground beef
1 teaspoon taco seasoning ✓
1 clove garlic, minced
1 cup whole kernel corn
1 ½ cups salsa ✓
1 cup milk ✓
1 tablespoon plain rice
    vinegar

½ cup sugar ✓
¼ cup butter ✓
1 egg
1 cup flour ✓
1 teaspoon baking powder
¼ teaspoon salt ✓
½ teaspoon baking soda
½ cup yellow corn meal

1. Preheat oven to 375 degrees F.
2. Brown beef in a large skillet. Add taco seasoning, garlic, corn and salsa. Bring to a boil. Reduce heat and simmer for 20 minutes. Pour into a greased 11x7 baking dish.
3. Meanwhile, pour vinegar into milk. Let stand for 5 minutes.
4. In a medium bowl cream together butter and sugar. Add eggs and mix well. Set aside.
5. In a small bowl combine flour, baking powder, salt and baking soda. Add to butter mixture. Slowly stir in milk mixture. Next add corn meal and stir until combined. Spread evenly over meat mixture. Bake for 25 minutes or until golden brown.

Hamburger Noodle Bake

This creamy and flavorful dish needs only a salad to make it a meal.

1 lb. ground beef
½ cup diced onion
½ teaspoon salt ✔
¼ teaspoon pepper
1 teaspoon sugar ✔
1 jar spaghetti sauce ✔
1 ½ cups sour cream ✔
3 oz. softened cream cheese
1 8oz. package egg noodles
½ cup shredded Cheddar cheese

1. Preheat oven to 350 degrees F.
2. In a large skillet brown beef and onions. Add salt, pepper, sugar and spaghetti sauce. Simmer for 20 minutes.
3. Meanwhile, cook noodles according to package.
4. In a small bowl mix sour cream and cream cheese.
5. In a 13x9 pan layer 1/3 of cooked noodles, meat mixture and sour cream mixture. Repeat 2 more times. Top with cheese. Bake for 25 minutes.

Hamburger Pie

This is an American classic that moms love because it sneaks in green beans and better yet, the kids love it too.

6 medium potatoes
4 tablespoons butter ✓
¼ cup milk ✓
½ teaspoon salt ✓
1 lb. ground beef
½ cup chopped onion
¼ teaspoon salt ✓
¼ teaspoon pepper
2 ½ cups frozen or canned beans
1 10½oz. can tomato soup
½ cup shredded Cheddar cheese

1. Peel potatoes, cut in half and place in a large pot of water. Heat on high and bring to a boil. Boil for 25 minutes or until potatoes are soft.
2. Drain potatoes, place in a mixer bowl and mix on low. Add butter, milk and ½ teaspoon salt. Mix on high for 30 seconds. Set aside.
3. Preheat oven to 350 degrees F.
4. In a large skillet, cook meat and onion until meat is brown and onion is tender. Stir in ¼ teaspoon salt, pepper, beans and soup. Pour into a greased 2-quart rectangular baking dish.
5. Spoon potato mixture on bean mixture. Sprinkle cheese over potatoes. Bake, uncovered 30 to 35 minutes or until mixture bubbles and cheese begins to brown.

Little Cheddar Meat Loaves

Leftovers make delicious meat loaf sandwiches.

1 egg
¾ cup milk ✔
1 cup shredded Cheddar cheese
½ cup quick cooking oatmeal
½ cup diced onion
1 teaspoon salt ✔
1 lb. ground beef
2/3 cup ketchup ✔
½ cup brown sugar ✔
1 ½ teaspoons mustard ✔

1. Preheat oven to 350 degrees F.
2. In a large bowl, beat egg and milk together. Stir in cheese oatmeal, onion and salt. Crumble in beef and mix well.
3. Shape into 8 mini loaves and place in a greased 13x9 pan.
4. In a small bowl mix together ketchup, brown sugar and mustard. Spoon sauce over loaves.
5. Bake uncovered for 45 minutes or until meat in no longer pink and internal temperature reaches at least 160 degrees F.

Meatballs

These basic meatballs can be used for spaghetti, stroganoff or appetizers.
Meatballs may be frozen before or after baking.

3 lbs. ground beef
3 large eggs, lightly beaten
½ cup milk ✓
4 slices of bread, processed to make bread crumbs
½ cup finely chopped onion
Salt ✓ and pepper
1 teaspoon optional spices – parsley, basil, oregano or thyme

1. Preheat oven to 425 degrees F.
2. Combine all ingredients. Shape into desired size meatballs and place on a 15x10 pan. Bake 25 minutes or until internal temperature reaches at least 160 degrees F. Makes 6 dozen small meatballs.

Salisbury Steak & Gravy

This is a spin on the old t.v. dinners that came with mashed potatoes and a mushy fruit dessert. It is a "lick your fingers clean" meal.

1 lb. ground beef
½ cup diced onion
1 teaspoon steak seasoning mix (I recommend *Montreal Seasoning* by McCormick)
2 tablespoons extra-virgin olive oil ✔
2 tablespoons butter ✔
10 chopped mushrooms
3 tablespoons flour ✔
2 cups beef broth ✔

1. In a bowl, mix together beef, onion and steak seasoning mix. Form 4 large 1 inch thick patties.
2. Heat 1 tablespoon olive oil in a large skillet over medium-high heat. Add meat patties. Cook 7 minutes on each side or until cooked through. Remove meat patties and cover with foil to keep warm.
3. Add 1 tablespoon olive oil, butter and mushrooms to skillet. Season with salt and pepper, and sauté for 5 minutes.
4. Add flour to mushrooms and cook for 2 minutes. Whisk in beef broth and thicken for 1 minute.
5. Serve mushroom gravy over beef patties.

Sloppy Joes

This American classic is better known as Sloppy Kennady's at our house. I always make this 1 day ahead of time to allow the flavors to blend.

1 tablespoon oil ✔
1 medium onion, minced
2 teaspoons minced garlic
¼ teaspoon chili powder
1 lb. ground beef
½ teaspoon salt ✔
¼ teaspoon pepper
2 teaspoons brown sugar ✔
½ cup tomato paste ✔
½ cup ketchup ✔
¼ cup water
4 hamburger buns

1. Heat oil in a large skillet over medium heat. Add onion and sauté until brown around the edges, about 5 minutes. Add garlic and chili powder and sauté for 30 seconds. Add beef, salt, pepper and brown sugar. Cook, using a wooden spoon to help break the meat into small pieces. Cook until no longer pink.
2. Add the tomato paste, ketchup and water. Simmer on low for 10 to 30 minutes. The longer the better. It's even better the next day.
3. Place ½ cup of meat mixture on each hamburger bun.

Spanish Rice

This rice tastes better than those from a box and it does not have the soy protein that is found in most rice boxes.

1 lb. ground beef
3 slices chopped bacon ✔
½ cup chopped onion
½ cup chopped green onions
1 16oz. canned diced tomatoes
2 cups water
1 cup long grain rice
½ cup chili sauce
1 tablespoon salt ✔
¼ teaspoon pepper

1. In a large skillet brown meat with the bacon, onion and green peppers.
2. Stir in undrained tomatoes, water, rice, chili sauce, salt and pepper. Bring to a boil and simmer for 30 minutes.

Stovetop Hamburger & Noodle Dish

This recipe is as convenient as the handy helper from a box, but without the MSG.

8 oz. rotelli
¾ lb. ground beef
½ cup chopped onion
1 14 ½oz. can chunky tomato sauce ✔
½ cup Parmesan cheese ✔
1 cup shredded Cheddar cheese

1. Cook noodles according to package and drain.
2. Meanwhile, in a large skillet brown beef and onion. Add tomato sauce and bring to a boil. Reduce heat and simmer for 4 minutes. Add pasta, Parmesan cheese and Cheddar cheese. Stir gently to coat pasta.

Stroganoff Meatballs

This is a nostalgic meal that will satisfy anyone's appetite. Serve with fresh green beans and applesauce to make it a meal.

2 cups beef broth ✔
¼ cup flour ✔
1 cup chopped onion
2 tablespoons melted butter ✔
30 precooked meatballs, fresh or frozen*
1 cup sour cream ✔

1. Combine beef broth and flour in a slow cooker, whisking until smooth. Add onion, butter and meatballs. Cover and cook on low for 4 to 5 hours.
2. Add sour cream and stir until blended. Cook on high for 30 minutes.
3. Serve over rice or noodles.

*I recommend using the meatball recipe found on page 40. I have been unable to purchase already made meatballs from the store because I found that they contained soy protein.

Stuffed Mexican Shells

My mom made this tasty dish for me as a teenager. It was so good that she probably never made it again because she was too busy trying more new recipes.

1 lb. ground beef
1 16oz. jar salsa ✔
1 8oz. can tomato sauce ✔
1 cup corn kernels
½ cup sliced black olives
12 oz. jumbo pasta shells (28 count), cooked, drained and cooled
1 cup shredded Cheddar cheese
1 cup sour cream ✔

1. Preheat oven to 375 degrees F.
2. Brown meat in a medium skillet. Stir in salsa, tomato sauce, corn and olives.
3. Stuff cooked pasta shells with 2 tablespoons of the meat mixture. Place in a lightly greased 13x9 pan. Sprinkle cheese on top of shells.
4. Bake for 20 minutes or until cheese is bubbly.
5. Serve with sour cream and salsa.

Stuffed Peppers

6 medium green peppers
1 lb. ground beef
1 small onion, chopped
1 teaspoon salt ✔
½ teaspoon pepper
1 ½ cups diced tomatoes
3 tablespoons salsa ✔
½ cup water
½ cup rice
1 cup grated Cheddar cheese

1. Wash and core peppers. Precook in boiling water for 5 minutes. Remove and drain.
2. In a large skillet cook beef, onion, salt and pepper until no longer pink. Add tomatoes, salsa, water and rice. Cover and simmer for 15 minutes or until rice is tender. Stir in cheese.
3. Preheat oven to 350 degrees F.
4. Stuff peppers with meat mixture and place upright in a baking dish. Bake uncovered for 25 minutes.

Sweet & Sour Meatballs

1 ½ lbs. ground beef
¾ cup quick cook oatmeal
1 egg
¼ cup chopped onion
½ teaspoon salt ✓
¼ teaspoon pepper
1 tablespoon oil ✓
1 20 oz. can pineapple chunks
1/3 cup water
3 tablespoons plain rice vinegar
1 teaspoon salt ✓
½ cup packed brown sugar ✓
3 tablespoons flour ✓
1 large green pepper, cut into 1-inch pieces
hot cooked rice

1. Mix beef, oatmeal, egg, onion, salt and pepper together. Shape into 1 inch balls. In a large skillet heat oil over medium heat. Add meatballs and cook until browned on all sides or until at least 160 degrees F. Turn frequently to brown all sides. Remove meatballs.
2. Drain pineapple, reserving juice. Set pineapple aside. Add water to juice if needed to measure 1 cup; pour into the meatball skillet. Add 1/3 cup water, vinegar, salt, brown sugar and flour; stir until smooth.
3. Cook over medium heat until thick, stirring constantly. Add the pineapple, meatballs and green pepper. Simmer, uncovered, for 20 minutes or until heated through. Serve with rice.

Tamale Pie

¾ cup yellow corn meal
1 ½ cups milk ✔
1 egg, beaten
1 lb. ground beef
1 ½ cups salsa ✔
1 tablespoon taco seasoning ✔
1 17oz. can whole kernel corn, drained
1 7½ oz. black olives, drained
1 cup shredded Cheddar cheese

1. Preheat oven to 350 degrees F.
2. In a 2 ½-quart casserole dish mix corn meal, milk and egg.
3. Brown meat in a skillet. Add salsa, taco seasoning, corn and olives.
4. Add meat mixture to corn meal mixture. Bake for 1 hour.
5. Sprinkle cheese on top and bake for 15 minutes or until cheese is bubbly.

Tortilla Casserole

1 lb. ground beef
1 cup chopped onion
1 14 ½ oz. can chunky tomato sauce ✔
2 tablespoons canned diced green chilies
8 – 6 inch corn tortillas ✔
2 cups shredded Cheddar cheese
Salsa ✔
Sour cream ✔

1. Preheat oven to 350 degrees F.
2. In a large skillet brown beef and onion. Add tomato sauce and green chilies.
3. Tear 4 corn tortillas into bite-sized pieces and place in a greased 7x11 baking dish. Add half the meat mixture. Then add 1 cup of Cheddar cheese. Repeat tortilla, meat and cheese layers.
4. Bake for 30 minutes.
5. Serve with salsa and sour cream.

Chicken

Apricot Salsa Chicken

This was a recipe given to me by my sister, Wendi. It is a great last minute meal you can throw together.

2 chicken breasts, cut into strips ✔
2 teaspoons oil ✔
2 tablespoons taco seasoning ✔
1 cup salsa ✔
1 cup apricot jam ✔
2 cups rice

1. Cook rice according to package.
2. In a skillet heat 2 teaspoons of oil over medium heat. Add chicken and cook through.
3. Add taco seasoning, salsa and jam. Simmer for 5 minutes.
4. Serve chicken mixture over rice.

Chicken & Broccoli Fettuccine

8 oz. fettuccine
2 boneless chicken breasts ✔
2 teaspoons extra-virgin olive oil ✔
2 cups broccoli flowerets
½ cup whipping cream ✔
1/3 cup Parmesan cheese ✔
1/8 teaspoon pepper
¼ teaspoon salt ✔

1. Cook fettuccine according to package.
2. Meanwhile, cut chicken into bite-size pieces and sauté in olive oil until golden brown.
3. 3 to 5 minutes before pasta is ready add broccoli. When done, drain and return to pot. Stir in cream, Parmesan cheese, pepper and salt. Add chicken.

Chicken & Vegetable Stir Fry

This is a great Chinese dish without the soy sauce. Serve this with Egg Drop soup for a complete meal.

3 cups cooked rice
2 boneless chicken breasts ✔
1 teaspoon minced garlic
2 tablespoons sesame oil
2 sliced carrots
2 sliced celery stalks
2 cups broccoli florets
2 sliced green onions
1 sliced red pepper
1 cup chicken broth ✔
4 tablespoons flour ✔

1. Cook rice according to package.
2. Meanwhile, cut chicken into bite size pieces.
3. In a large skillet over medium-high heat, sauté chicken and garlic in 1 tablespoon of oil until chicken is completely cooked. Add 1 tablespoon of oil and vegetables. Sauté until vegetables are crisp-tender.
4. In a small bowl, whisk broth and flour together. Reduce heat to medium and pour chicken broth mixture over chicken mixture. Cook until thickened.
5. Serve over rice.

Chicken Casserole

1 cup wild rice
½ cup chopped onion
½ cup butter ✔
½ cup flour ✔
6 oz. can mushrooms
1 cup chicken broth ✔
¾ cup cream ✔
¾ cup milk ✔
3 cups diced cooked chicken or turkey ✔
2 tablespoons dried parsley
1 ½ teaspoons salt ✔
¼ teaspoon pepper
½ cup sliced almonds

1. Cook rice according to package.
2. Preheat oven to 350 degrees F.
3. Sauté onions in butter until soft. Remove from heat and stir in flour. Set aside.
4. Drain mushrooms, reserving liquid. Add chicken broth to mushroom liquid to make 1 ½ cups. Add liquids to onions and cook over medium-low. Slowly add cream and milk. Stir until thickened.
5. Mix together onion mixture, rice, mushrooms, chicken, parsley, salt and pepper. Place in a 2-quart casserole dish. Sprinkle almonds on top. Bake uncovered for 30 minutes or until hot.

Chicken Divan

1 lb. chopped broccoli (about 4 cups)
6 cups cooked chicken, shredded ✔
2 cups mayonnaise
2 cups sour cream ✔
1 cup grated sharp Cheddar cheese
1 tablespoon fresh lemon juice
1 teaspoon curry powder
1 teaspoon minced onions
Salt ✔ and pepper
½ cup chicken broth ✔
½ cup freshly grated Parmesan cheese ✔
½ cup soft bread crumbs
2 tablespoons butter, melted ✔

1. Preheat oven to 350 degrees F.
2. Place broccoli and chicken in a 13x9 casserole dish.
3. In a medium bowl, combine the mayonnaise, sour cream, Cheddar cheese, lemon juice, curry powder, minced onion, salt and pepper, to taste, and broth. Whisk together to make a sauce. Pour the sauce over the broccoli and chicken. Mix well with a spatula.
4. Place the mixture into a 9x13 casserole dish or two 9-inch square pans that have been sprayed with vegetable oil cooking spray. Pat down evenly and smooth with a spatula. Combine the Parmesan cheese, bread crumbs and butter and sprinkle over the top.
5. Bake for 30 to 45 minutes.

Chicken Enchiladas

What is not to love about a chicken enchilada? I love anything topped with cheese and sour cream.

1 tablespoon butter ✔
1/3 cup chopped onion
3 cups shredded cooked chicken ✔
1 14oz. can stewed tomatoes
½ cup salsa ✔
¼ teaspoon chili powder
¼ teaspoon salt ✔
1 10oz. can green chili enchilada sauce
10 – 6 inch flour tortillas ✔
½ cup sour cream ✔
¾ cup shredded Cheddar cheese

1. Preheat oven to 450 degrees F.
2. In a large skillet melt butter. Add onion and sauté until soft. Add chicken, tomatoes, ¼ cup salsa, chili powder and salt. Heat through and keep warm.
3. Place half of the enchilada sauce in a 13x9 pan. Place ¼ cup of chicken mixture on each tortilla. Roll up each tortilla and place in 13x9 pan. Top with remaining enchilada sauce, salsa, sour cream and cheese. Cover with foil, bake for 30 minutes or until cheese is melted.

Chicken Linguine with Pesto

8 oz. linguine
2 boneless chicken breasts ✔
1 tablespoon extra-virgin olive oil ✔
½ cup pesto (recipe found on page 127)
2 large diced Roma tomatoes
¼ cup Parmesan cheese ✔

1. Cook pasta according to package. Drain and return to pan.
2. Meanwhile cut chicken into narrow strips. Heat oil in a medium skillet and cook chicken over medium-high heat. Stir in pesto and tomatoes. Add pasta and toss to mix. Cook over low heat until heated through.
3. Garnish with Parmesan cheese.

Chicken Nuggets

This is a healthier option to the fast food versions that can contain MSG.

¼ cup butter ✔
2 garlic cloves, minced
1 cup fine bread crumbs
¼ cup freshly grated Parmesan cheese ✔
2 boneless chicken breasts, cut into 1-inch cubes ✔

1. Preheat the oven to 400 degrees F.
2. In a small saucepan melt butter with the garlic and let the mixture cool slightly.
3. In a shallow bowl or pie plate toss the crumbs with the Parmesan cheese. Dip the chicken cubes first in the butter and then in the bread crumb mixture, making sure that each cube is coated well with crumbs. Arrange the chicken in one layer on a baking sheet and bake 15 minutes or until the chicken is just cooked through. Transfer to paper towels to drain.

Chicken Pesto & Angel Hair Pasta

16 oz. angel hair pasta
2 cups whipping cream ✔
½ cup pesto (recipe found on page 127)
1 tablespoon extra-virgin olive oil ✔
3 garlic cloves, minced
1 lb. chicken breasts cut into strips ✔

1. Cook pasta according to package. Drain and return to pot.
2. Meanwhile, place whipping cream in a small saucepan. Bring to a boil. Stir in pesto, remove from heat and set aside.
3. Heat olive oil in a large skillet. Add garlic and sauté for 1 minute. Add chicken strips and cook until lightly browned. Stir in pesto sauce and bring to a simmer. Add pasta and toss to mix.

Chicken Pot Pie

2 teaspoons extra-virgin olive oil ✓
½ cup chopped onion
2 boneless chicken breast, cut into 1 inch cubes, about 2 cups ✓
2 tablespoons flour ✓
1 teaspoon dried thyme
½ teaspoon salt ✓
¼ teaspoon ground black pepper
¼ teaspoon paprika
2 carrots, peeled and chopped
2 celery stalks, chopped
4 medium red potatoes cut into ½ inch cubes
1 14 ½oz. can crushed tomatoes
1 cup chicken broth ✓
¼ cup water
1 teaspoon Dijon mustard ✓
½ cup frozen corn kernels
1 9-inch frozen pie crust, thawed
1 egg, lightly beaten

1. Preheat oven to 425 degrees F.
2. Heat oil in a large oven-proof stockpot over medium heat. Add onion and sauté 2 minutes. Add chicken and sauté 5 to 7 minutes, until browned on all sides.
3. In a small bowl, combine flour, thyme, salt, pepper and paprika. Add flour mixture to the chicken and stir to coat. Stir in carrots, celery, potatoes, tomatoes, chicken broth, water and Dijon mustard and mix well. Bring mixture to a boil. Cook until vegetables are tender.
4. Transfer stew to a 2-quart casserole dish and stir in corn. Place pie crust on top of casserole and pinch around the

edges to seal the crust to the dish. Brush the top with egg and prick the surface 2 times with a sharp knife to allow steam to escape during cooking. Place casserole dish on baking sheet and bake 8 to 10 minutes, until crust is golden.

Creamy Apricot Chicken with Noodles

4 boneless chicken breasts ✔
¼ cup butter ✔
1 tablespoon Dijon mustard ✔
½ cup sour cream ✔
½ cup apricot jam ✔
10 oz. egg noodles
1 tablespoon extra-virgin olive oil ✔
2 tablespoons sliced, toasted almonds

1. Preheat oven to 375 degrees F.
2. Place chicken in an 8x8 baking dish. Pour ¼ cup melted butter over chicken. Bake for 25 minutes. Baste once.
3. Combine mustard, sour cream and apricot jam. Remove chicken from the oven and pour sauce over top. Bake 25 minutes or until chicken is cooked through.
4. Cook noodles according to package. Drain and toss with 1 tablespoon olive oil. Serve chicken over noodles and sprinkle with toasted almonds.

Creamy Chicken Enchiladas

3 ½ cups sour cream ✔
2 cups cooked chicken, shredded ✔
1 4oz. can chilies, drained
1/3 cup onion flakes
1 teaspoon chili powder
½ teaspoon salt ✔
¼ teaspoon pepper
10 – 6 inch tortillas ✔
2 cups shredded Cheddar cheese

1. Preheat oven at 450 degrees F.
2. Spread 1 cup of sour cream in a 13x9 baking dish.
3. In a 2-quart saucepan mix chicken, ½ cup sour cream, chilies, onion flakes, chili powder, salt and pepper. Cook over low heat, stirring occasionally until heated.
4. Place ¼ cup of chicken mixture into each tortilla. Roll tortilla and place seam side down in a 13x9 baking dish. Continue until all tortillas are filled. Spread remaining sour cream over tortillas and sprinkle with cheese.
5. Bake for 10 minutes or until cheese is melted.

Curry & Chutney Chicken

3 cups rice
½ cup chopped onion
1 tablespoon sugar ✔
1 teaspoon curry powder
1 teaspoon ground coriander
¼ teaspoon ground cinnamon
1/8 teaspoon cayenne pepper
½ teaspoon turmeric
½ teaspoon kosher salt ✔
1 pinch ground cloves
½ cup diced tomatoes
6 4oz. boneless chicken breasts, cut into thirds ✔
½ cup chutney (recipes can be found on page 108, 118 & 126)
1/3 cup chopped cashews(optional)

1. Cook rice according to package.
2. Meanwhile, in a large bowl combine all ingredients and stir to combine. Heat a skillet over medium heat and cook mixture for 20 minutes or until chicken is cooked through.
3. Serve over rice and sprinkle with chopped cashews if desired.

Fajitas

This recipe has all the flavor without the soy protein that is often found in seasoning packets. This is my husband's favorite meal.

1/3 cup extra-virgin olive oil ✔
2 garlic cloves, minced
2 teaspoons taco seasoning ✔
2 chicken breasts ✔ or 1 lb. petite sirloin
1 sliced sweet onion
1 sliced red bell pepper
1/3 cup water
2 teaspoons taco seasoning ✔
8 – 6 inch flour tortillas ✔
3 cups shredded Cheddar cheese
Salsa ✔
Sour cream ✔

1. In a small bowl mix olive oil, garlic and 2 teaspoons taco seasoning. Set marinade aside. Slice meat into strips. Place meat and 1/3 cup of marinade into a self seal bag. Seal bag and place in refrigerator for at least 30 minutes.
2. Slice onion and red bell pepper into ¼ inch thick slices. Set aside. In a medium skillet, heat 2 teaspoons olive oil over medium heat. Add onion and red bell pepper. Cook until onion is soft. Remove and set aside.
3. Remove meat from marinade. Cook meat in skillet over medium heat until no longer pink. Discard used marinade. Mix together water and 2 teaspoons taco seasoning. Add onion, pepper and taco seasoning mixture to meat. Bring to a boil and simmer for 5 minutes.
4. To serve, place meat and vegetables in tortillas. Top with salsa, shredded cheese and sour cream.

Fried Chicken & Gravy

MSG is often the secret spice in store bought fried chicken. This recipe is the ultimate comfort food.

Fried Chicken

1 chicken, cut up ✔   ½ cup flour ✔

Salt ✔ and pepper   Oil ✔

1. Rinse chicken, but do not dry. Sprinkle with salt and pepper. Roll chicken in flour and shake off excess.
2. Heat 2 inches of oil in a deep 12 inch cast iron skillet or chicken fryer. Temperature of oil should be 350 degrees F.
3. Add chicken, skin side down. Cover and cook 10 minutes. Uncover and cook 5 minutes or until golden brown. Flip and cook uncovered for 10 minutes or until golden brown and cooked through.

Gravy

4 tablespoons fat from frying chicken

4 tablespoons flour ✔

½ cup heavy cream ✔

1 ½ cups water

Salt ✔ and pepper

1. Leave 4 tablespoons chicken fat in skillet and the crusty bits that stick to the bottom. Add flour and stir until blended. Cook until lightly browned, stirring constantly.
2. Gradually stir in cream and water. Continue cooking and stir frequently until thickened, about 5 minutes. Salt and pepper to taste.
3. If gravy is too thick stir in milk. If too thin add a little flour mixed with water.

Honey Chicken

6 boneless chicken breasts ✔
¼ cup butter ✔
½ cup good-quality honey
¼ cup yellow mustard ✔
1 teaspoon curry powder

1. Preheat the oven at 375 degrees F.
2. Melt butter and pour into a 13x9 pan. Stir in honey, mustard and curry.
3. Roll the chicken in the mixture and lay in pan.
4. Bake for 1 hour.

Mock Chicken Cordon Bleu

This is an easier version that doesn't require the time or patience to prepare it.

4 boneless chicken breasts ✔
1 cup white bread crumbs
½ teaspoon salt ✔
½ teaspoon thyme
¼ cup sour cream ✔
4 thin slices of ham ✔
4 thin slices Swiss cheese

1. Preheat oven to 350 degrees F.
2. Combine bread crumbs, salt and thyme. Brush chicken with sour cream. Roll chicken in crumbs to coat. Place chicken in a greased baking dish. Bake for 30 to 40 minutes or until cooked through.
3. Top each chicken with a ham slice folded to fit. Top with cheese slices. Bake long enough to melt cheese.

Peanut Chicken Stir-Fry

My kids love this dish and I love how easy it is.

2 cups rice
¾ cup chicken broth ✔
¼ cup creamy peanut butter ✔
1 teaspoon salt ✔
¼ teaspoon pepper
½ teaspoon ground ginger
4 teaspoons flour ✔
1 lb. boneless chicken breasts, cut into bite size strips ✔
3 teaspoons extra-virgin olive oil ✔
1 cup chopped onion
1 cup chopped green pepper
1 cup chopped red pepper
1 ½ cups sliced mushrooms
1 teaspoon minced garlic

1. Cook rice according to package.
2. Meanwhile, in a small bowl, combine the next six ingredients until smooth. Set aside.
3. Heat 1 ½ teaspoons olive oil in a large skillet over medium heat. Add chicken and cook for 5 minutes or until no longer pink. Remove with a slotted spoon and set aside.
4. Add 1 ½ teaspoons olive oil to the large skillet over medium heat. Add onions and peppers and cook for 5 minutes. Add mushrooms and garlic and cook for 3 to 4 minutes longer or until vegetables are crisp-tender.
5. Stir flour mixture and add to the pan. Bring to a boil and cook for 2 minutes. Stirring constantly. Add chicken and heat through. Serve with rice.

Ranch Chicken & Pasta

8 oz. egg noodles
½ cup butter ✔
2 teaspoons ranch seasoning ✔
½ cup peas
½ cup freshly grated Parmesan cheese ✔
2 cups cubed cooked chicken ✔

1. Cook noodles according to package, drain and return to pot.
2. Meanwhile, melt butter in a small saucepan. Add ranch seasoning. Add butter sauce and ¼ cup cheese to the pasta. Toss to coat. Add chicken and peas. Toss to coat.
3. To serve sprinkle with ¼ cup cheese.

Sweet & Sour Chicken

A lot of savory chicken in an easy to make meal.

1 cup ketchup ✓
¾ cup plain rice vinegar
1 ½ teaspoons mustard ✓
1 ½ cups brown sugar ✓
½ teaspoon minced garlic
1 tablespoon minced dried onions
1/8 teaspoon celery salt
3 boneless chicken breasts ✓

1. Preheat oven to 350 degrees F.
2. In a small sauce pan combine ketchup, vinegar, mustard, brown sugar, garlic, dried onion and celery salt. Bring to boil. Reduce heat and simmer for 30 minutes
3. Place chicken in a greased 13x9 pan. Pour sauce over chicken. Bake for 30 minutes. Flip chicken and bake for 30 minutes. Basting frequently with sauce.

Pork

Apricot Pineapple Pork Chops

1 tablespoon butter ✔
1 lb. boneless pork chops ✔
1 teaspoon butter ✔
½ cup apricot pineapple jam ✔
2 sliced green onions
½ teaspoon dry mustard
1 tablespoon plain rice vinegar

1. Heat 1 tablespoon butter in a skillet over medium-high heat. Add pork chops. Sauté the pork chops for 5 minutes per side or until cooked through. Remove pork chops from the skillet.
2. Add 1 teaspoon of butter, jam, green onions, dry mustard and vinegar to the skillet. Mix, cover and simmer for 4 minutes.
3. Add the pork chops. Cook until the pork chops are heated through.

Biscuits & Gravy

This is a dish that people often think of when you say "comfort food." It's a great basic recipe.

1 lb. ground sausage ✔
4 tablespoons flour ✔
4 tablespoons butter ✔
1 teaspoon salt ✔
1 teaspoon pepper
4 cups milk ✔
6 biscuits or toast

1. In a deep skillet brown sausage over medium heat. Add flour, butter, salt and pepper. Next gradually add milk. Bring to a boil. Boil on medium-low for 2 minutes.
2. Serve over biscuits or toast.

Creamy Herbed Pork Chops

4 pork chops
1 tablespoon butter ✔
1/3 cup finely chopped carrot
¼ teaspoon pepper
1 tablespoon chopped parsley
4 teaspoons flour ✔
½ teaspoon dried basil
2/3 cup cream or milk ✔
2 tablespoons water

1. Place butter and pork chops in a large skillet. Salt and pepper to taste. Cook over medium heat for 5 minutes. Turn pork chops and add carrot. Cook for 5 to 7 minutes more or until no longer pink. Remove pork chops and set aside.

2. Stir parsley, flour, basil and pepper into the drippings and carrot. Add cream/milk all at once. Cook and stir until sauce thickens and is bubbly. Add water and stir. Return pork chops to skillet and heat through.

Curry Rice

This is not a new recipe but a twist on an old favorite, fried rice. It makes leftover ham go a long way.

2 cups brown long grain rice
4 cups chicken broth ✓
1 tablespoon butter ✓
½ teaspoon curry
¼ teaspoon salt ✓
1 cup diced ham ✓
1 egg
½ cup frozen peas

1. In a large pot mix rice, broth, butter, curry and salt. Heat over high and bring to a boil. Stirring occasionally. Simmer on low for 60 minutes.
2. In a small skillet brown ham over medium heat. Set aside in a small bowl.
3. In the same skillet scramble one egg in a small amount of butter. Add to ham bowl.
4. When rice is done add ham, egg and peas. Stir until all ingredients are warm.

Ham & Egg Rolls

This recipe was one of my first 4-H food demonstrations at the Northwest Washington Fair in Lynden, Washington. It won blue ribbon and qualified for the State Fair.

3 tablespoons butter ✔
3 ½ tablespoons flour ✔
2 cups hot milk ✔
3 teaspoons chopped parsley
6 hard boiled eggs, sliced
1 lb. broccoli, cooked, drained and chopped
14 thin slices of ham ✔
½ cup shredded Cheddar cheese
Salt ✔ and pepper

1. Place butter in a medium glass dish. Microwave until butter is melted. Whisk in flour. Microwave 2 minutes uncovered. Whisk in milk and 1 teaspoon parsley. Microwave for 1 ½ minutes and stir. Repeat two more times.
2. Preheat oven to 375 degrees F.
3. Place eggs and broccoli in a medium bowl and toss to mix. Add half of the white sauce and mix well. Place 2 tablespoons of egg mixture on each ham slice. Roll and place seam side down in a greased 8x10 dish. Pour remaining white sauce over ham and sprinkle with cheese. Salt and pepper to taste.
4. Bake for 8 minutes or until cheese is melted.

Ham Balls

This recipe is in memory of Arie VanWeerdhuizen and all the great MSG free meats he sold at his small town meat shop in Lynden, Washington.

1 lb. ground ham ✔
1 lb. ground pork or beef ✔
1 cup bread crumbs
1 egg
½ cup milk ✔
1 10½oz. can tomato soup
1 cup brown sugar ✔
1 teaspoon dry mustard
2 tablespoons plain rice vinegar

1. Preheat oven to 350 degrees F.
2. In a large bowl mix ham, pork/beef, bread crumbs, egg and milk. Shape into 30 balls and place in a 13x9 pan.
3. In a medium bowl mix together tomato soup, sugar, mustard and vinegar. Spoon over ham balls. Cover and bake for 1 hour.

Ham Loaf

1 lb. ground ham ✔
1 lb. ground beef
¾ cup bread crumbs
1 egg
¼ cup finely chopped onion
½ cup milk ✔

1. Preheat oven to 350 degrees F.
2. Combine ham, beef, bread crumbs, egg, onion and milk in a mixing bowl.
3. Spoon mixture into a lightly greased 8x8 baking dish. Form into a loaf, about 6x7 inches in size. Bake for 45 to 60 minutes or to 160 degrees F.

Honey Glazed Pork Chops

6 boneless pork chops ✔
½ cup good-quality honey
3 tablespoons plain rice vinegar
1 teaspoon salt ✔
½ teaspoon dry mustard
1 large apple, peeled and sliced
½ cup raisins
2 tablespoons brown sugar ✔

1. Preheat oven to 325 degrees F.
2. Place the pork chops in a 13x9 pan.
3. Mix together honey, vinegar, salt and mustard. Pour mixture over pork chops. Top with apples and raisins. Sprinkle with brown sugar.
4. Bake for 1 hour, basting occasionally with the pan juices.

Vegetables & Pasta

Autumn Wild Rice

2 cups wild rice
2 teaspoons salt ✔
1 ½ cups sliced mushrooms
½ cup sliced water chestnuts
4 tablespoons butter ✔
½ cup cashews ✔

1. Bring 6 cups of water to a boil. Add rice and salt. Cover and simmer for 60 minutes. Drain.
2. Sauté rice in 2 tablespoons of butter.
3. In a separate pan sauté mushrooms and water chestnuts in remaining butter.
4. Combine rice, mushroom mixture and cashews.

Broccoli with Cheese Sauce

An old fashion favorite that will even fool my husband into eating broccoli.

1 ¼ pounds broccoli, cut into bite size pieces
3 tablespoons butter ✓
¼ cup flour ✓
1 cup heavy cream ✓
½ cup water
½ cup Cheddar cheese
Salt ✓ and pepper to taste

1. Steam broccoli until crisp-tender.
2. Meanwhile, melt butter in a medium saucepan. Quickly stir in flour and cook for 1 minute. Remove from heat. Gradually stir in cream and water until smooth. Cook over medium-low heat, stirring frequently, until thickened.
3. Reduce heat and gradually stir in cheese until melted. Add salt and pepper to taste.
4. Place broccoli in a serving dish and top with the sauce.

Cheesy Potatoes

This is the recipe this cookbook was written for. It is one of my favorite comfort foods without the MSG from a cream of yummy soup.

2 lbs. frozen shredded hash browns
½ teaspoon pepper
2 teaspoons salt ✔
2 tablespoons dried minced onion
2 cups sour cream ✔
3 cups Cheddar cheese
2 cups corn flakes ✔
¼ cup melted butter ✔

1. Preheat the oven to 350 degrees F.
2. In a large bowl, mix the hash browns, pepper, salt, dried onion, sour cream and 2 cups of Cheddar cheese. Pour into the 13x9 pan.
3. In a medium bowl, mix 1 cup cheese, corn flakes and melted butter. Sprinkle on top of hash brown mixture.
4. Bake covered for 1 ½ hours and ½ hour uncovered.

Cheesy Rice

1 ¾ cups long grain rice
1 cup finely chopped onion
1/3 cup melted butter ✔
1 ½ cups shredded Cheddar cheese
4 cups chicken broth ✔
¼ cup sliced almonds ✔

1. Preheat oven to 350 degrees F.
2. Combine all ingredients in a large mixing bowl. Pour into a greased 2-quart casserole dish.
3. Bake for 1 ½ hours or until liquids are absorbed.

Cornbread Casserole

My sister-in-law, Karen, gave me this family recipe. A variation on a traditional cornbread that gets its smooth taste from sour cream. This is great with taco soup.

2 cups flour ✓
1 ½ cups yellow cornmeal
2 tablespoons baking powder
2 teaspoons salt ✓
2 cups milk ✓
2 large eggs
2/3 cup sugar ✓
2 tablespoons melted butter ✓
1 14.75oz. can creamed corn
¼ cup butter ✓
1 cup shredded Cheddar cheese
2 cups sour cream ✓

1. Preheat the oven to 400 degrees F.
2. In a large bowl, mix the flour, cornmeal, baking powder and salt. Set aside.
3. Whisk together milk, eggs, sugar and 2 tablespoons melted butter in a small bowl. Stir in creamed corn. Fold the wet ingredients into the dry ingredients until combined.
4. Pour into a greased 13x9 pan.
5. Cut butter into 8 pieces and place on corn bread mixture.
6. Sprinkle cheese on next.
7. Place dollops of sour cream on top.
8. Bake uncovered for 45 minutes, until edges are golden brown.

Fettuccine Alfredo

16 oz. fettuccine
½ cup butter ✔
1 cup heavy whipping cream ✔
1 cup grated Parmesan cheese ✔
Salt ✔ and pepper to taste

1. Cook pasta as directed on package, drain.
2. While pasta is cooking, melt butter in a saucepan over low heat. Slowly add cream and continuously stir until heated through. Add cheese and continuously stir until cheese is completely melted.
3. Add cooked pasta to sauce and stir until noodles are coated. Salt and pepper to taste.

Scalloped Potatoes

This recipe takes little effort to make yummy creamy potatoes. Bake it now or place it the fridge until later.

3 tablespoons butter ✔
2 tablespoons flour ✔
1 ½ teaspoons salt ✔
¼ teaspoon pepper
3 cups milk ✔
6 medium potatoes, thinly sliced
2 teaspoons diced onions
1 lb. diced ham

1. Preheat oven to 350 degrees F.
2. In a medium bowl combine butter, flour, salt, pepper and milk for the white sauce. Set aside.
3. Place half the potatoes, ham and onion in a greased 3-quart casserole dish. Cover with half the white sauce. Layer the remaining potatoes, onions and ham. Cover with the remaining white sauce.
4. Cover and bake for 1 hour. Uncover and bake for 20 minutes or until browned.

Tuna & Noodles

A newer version of tuna casserole without the MSG.

8 oz. egg noodles
¼ cup butter ✔
¼ cup flour ✔
1 teaspoon salt ✔
¼ teaspoon pepper
2 cups milk ✔
1/3 cup sharp Cheddar cheese
2 cups frozen peas & carrots
2 6oz. cans of tuna, drained ✔
1 cup crushed plain potato chips ✔
2 tablespoons melted butter ✔

1. Cook noodles according to package and drain.
2. Preheat oven to 400 degrees F.
3. Meanwhile, melt butter in a medium saucepan. Stir in flour, salt and pepper. Whisk briskly, cooking over medium-high heat, until mixture begins to darken, two to five minutes. Remove from heat. Add milk and stir to blend. Return to heat and continue cooking until thickened. Stir frequently. Turn off heat and add cheese. Stir until cheese is melted. Add noodles, peas, carrots and tuna.
4. Place in greased 3-quart baking dish. Mix potato chips and 2 tablespoons of butter. Sprinkle chips over noodle mixture. Bake uncovered for 25 minutes.

White and Wild Rice

This rice tastes better than those from a box and it does not have the soy protein that is found in most rice boxes.

2 cups chicken broth ✔
3 tablespoons wild rice
1 cup white rice
2 tablespoons butter ✔
2 tablespoons chopped chives (optional)

1. In a medium sauce pan bring broth to a boil. Add wild rice, white rice and butter. Return to boil. Stir, cover and reduce heat to medium-low. Simmer for 20 minutes or until tender.
2. Add chives if desired and fluff with a fork.

Variations
➢ Add ½ teaspoon parsley to chicken broth.
➢ Sauté 1 tablespoon butter, ¼ cup chopped onions and 2 tablespoons sliced almonds. Add to broth.

Salads

Asian Salad with Sesame Dressing

Sesame dressing

2 tablespoons plain rice vinegar

1 shallot , quartered

½ teaspoon salt ✓

1/8 teaspoon pepper

2 teaspoons peanut butter ✓

1 tablespoon sesame seeds

½ cup sesame oil

Salad

6 cups salad mix of assorted small, young salad leaves

1 8oz. can mandarin oranges, drained

1 red bell pepper, stem and seeds removed and sliced julienne

1 4oz. can water chestnuts, rinsed

1 cup cherry tomatoes, halved

1. Add 1 at a time through the feed tube of a food processor, vinegar, shallot, salt, pepper, peanut butter and sesame seeds. Leaving the food processor running add the oil in a slow thin stream. Set aside.

2. Toss greens, oranges, bell pepper, water chestnuts and tomatoes together in a large bowl with enough dressing to coat. Serve with additional dressing on the side.

Coleslaw

This traditional recipe is a great addition to any light dinner or lunch.

1 tablespoon Dijon mustard ✔
1 tablespoon apple cider vinegar
1 tablespoon fresh lemon juice
1 tablespoon sugar ✔
1 teaspoon salt ✔
½ cup mayonnaise
¼ cup sour cream ✔
1 small green cabbage, finely shredded
2 medium carrots, cut in 1/8 inch matchsticks

1. In a small bowl whisk together the mustard, vinegar, lemon juice, sugar, salt, mayonnaise and sour cream.
2. Place cabbage and carrots in a large bowl. Pour the dressing over and toss to coat. Cover and refrigerate until the slaw softens. About 2 hours. Before serving toss the coleslaw again.

Festive Fruit Salad

1 20oz. can pineapple chunks
½ cup sugar ✔
3 tablespoons flour ✔
1 egg, lightly beaten
1 15oz. can mandarin oranges, drained
1 20oz. can pears, drained and chopped
3 kiwi, peeled and sliced
2 large chopped apples
1 cup pecan halves

1. Drain pineapple, reserving juice. Set pineapple aside and pour juice into a small saucepan. Add sugar and flour. Bring to a boil and stir constantly. Quickly stir in egg. Cook until thick. Cool in refrigerator.
2. In a large bowl, combine pineapple chunks, mandarin oranges, pears, kiwi, apples and pecans. Pour dressing over and stir until fruit is coated. Cover and chill 1 hour before serving.

Grilled Veggies

½ bunch asparagus, trimmed and cut into bite-size pieces
1 pint cherry tomatoes
1 medium red onion, cut into ½ inch rings
1 yellow bell pepper, quartered, seeds and ribs removed
1 red bell pepper, quartered, seeds and ribs removed
¼ cup extra-virgin olive oil, for brushing ✔
Salt ✔ and freshly ground black pepper
¼ cup fresh basil leaves

Dressing
1 medium garlic clove, minced
1 tablespoon plain rice vinegar
3 tablespoons extra-virgin olive oil ✔
Salt ✔ and freshly ground black pepper

1. Preheat grill to medium.
2. In a large bowl, toss the vegetables with olive oil and season with salt and pepper. Grill the vegetables, turning occasionally, until charred and tender, about 5 to 7 minutes. Remove to a platter. Sprinkle with basil.
3. In a small bowl, mix garlic, vinegar and olive oil. Season with salt and pepper and drizzle over vegetables.

Mango & Red Onion Salad

This recipe is so easy, yet so flavorful. The cumin gives the salad an exotic flair.

2 cups cubed fresh mango
½ cup halved cherry tomatoes
2 tablespoons minced red onion
2 tablespoons fresh lime juice
½ teaspoon ground cumin
Salt ✔ and pepper

In a medium bowl, combine mango, tomatoes, onion, lime juice and cumin. Toss to combine. Season, to taste, with salt and pepper.

Pomegranate Salad

This salad takes a little effort but the finished product is well worth the extra preparation. It will impress all your guests at your next party.

2 tablespoons pomegranate juice
1 teaspoon grated orange zest
¼ cup apple cider vinegar
2 shallots, minced
1 teaspoon salt ✔
½ teaspoon freshly ground black pepper
1 tablespoon Dijon mustard ✔
½ cup extra-virgin olive oil ✔
3 oranges, peeled and segmented
1 small red onion, thinly sliced
8 ounces mozzarella cheese, cut crosswise into 6 slices
6 thin slices prosciutto
12 cups mixed greens

1. In a small bowl, combine the pomegranate juice, orange zest, vinegar, shallots, salt, pepper and mustard and whisks thoroughly to combine. Add the oil in a steady stream and whisk until emulsified. Fold the segmented oranges and sliced onions into ¼ cup of the dressing and toss to combine and set aside.
2. Wrap each slice of cheese in a slice of prosciutto. Heat a large skillet over medium-high heat. Add the wrapped cheeses and sear on both sides. Remove from the heat.
3. In a large salad bowl, combine greens, oranges and onion. Toss gently with enough dressing to coat. Divide among salad plates and top with a seared cheese package and pomegranate seeds. Spoon a little dressing over each salad.

Roasted Sweet Potato Salad

A new way to serve sweet potatoes and a great way to use up those fall pumpkin seeds.

Salad:

4 medium sweet potatoes, peeled and cut into 1-inch pieces
5 tablespoons extra-virgin olive oil ✔
1 tablespoon finely chopped fresh rosemary
1 teaspoon salt, plus more as needed ✔
1 teaspoon freshly ground black pepper, plus more as needed
½ teaspoon ground cumin
½ teaspoon ground ginger
1 cup raw green pumpkin seeds
1 cup dried cranberries
1 cup chopped scallions (green and white)
1 cup julienned roasted red pepper

Dressing

6 tablespoons apple cider vinegar
1/3 cup mango chutney or Hawaiian Chutney found on page 118
2 tablespoons Dijon mustard ✔
2 tablespoons good-quality honey
2 garlic cloves, minced
¼ cup extra-virgin olive oil ✔

1. Preheat oven to 425 degrees F.
2. In a roasting pan, combine the potatoes, 3 tablespoons of the olive oil, rosemary, salt, pepper, cumin and ginger. Stir to combine and bake until the potatoes are fork-tender and golden brown, about 25 to 30 minutes.
3. Meanwhile, heat the remaining 2 tablespoons olive oil in a skillet over medium-high heat. Add the pumpkin seeds

and cook, stirring, until toasted. Transfer the seeds to a plate and season with salt and pepper.

4. In a small bowl, combine the cranberries, scallions and red pepper and set aside.
5. Prepare the dressing by combining all the ingredients (except for the olive oil) in a small saucepan and heat. Remove from heat and whisk in the olive oil. Assemble salad by gently tossing the potatoes with the pepper mixture. Add enough of the dressing to coat and garnish with toasted pumpkin seeds. Serve with extra dressing on the side.

Seven Layer Salad

No Christian Reformed Church potluck is complete without this salad.

1 head iceberg or romaine lettuce, chopped
½ cup chopped celery
¼ cup chopped green onions
1 4oz. can sliced water chestnuts, drained and rinsed
1 cup frozen peas
2 cups mayonnaise
1 tablespoon sugar ✔
1 diced tomato
½ cup bacon bits ✔
3 hard boiled eggs, chopped
¼ teaspoon salt ✔
¼ teaspoon pepper
2 cups shredded Cheddar cheese

1. Place half the lettuce in a 13x9 dish or trifle bowl.
2. Top with celery, green onions, water chestnut and peas.
3. Place the remaining lettuce in the dish.
4. Spread mayonnaise evenly over the top of the salad. Sprinkle with sugar.
5. Top with tomatoes, bacon, eggs, salt, pepper and cheese.
6. Cover with plastic wrap and chill for at least 8 hours.

Spinach & Raspberry Salad

This glamorous salad is lovely with raspberries, but can also be made with strawberries, blueberries or cranberries.

1 large bag spinach
½ cup sugar ✔
1 ½ tablespoons sesame seeds
1 tablespoon poppy seeds
1 ½ teaspoons minced onion
¼ teaspoon salt ✔
½ teaspoon paprika
¼ cup oil ✔
¼ cup apple cider vinegar
½ cup grated Parmesan cheese ✔
1 quart raspberries (or sliced strawberries, blueberries or dried cranberries)

1. Place sugar, sesame seeds, poppy seeds, onion, salt and paprika in a jar and stir well. Add oil and vinegar. Shake well.
2. Place spinach in a large bowl. Toss with dressing. Sprinkle with raspberries and Parmesan cheese.

Sweet & Sour Spinach Salad

1 head of spinach or 1 bag
1 tablespoon plain rice vinegar
1 tablespoon sugar ✔
¼ cup mayonnaise
1 small read onion, thinly sliced rings
8 slices bacon, cooked & crumbled ✔
1 15oz. can mandarin oranges, drained

1. Wash spinach and dry. Remove stems and tear into bite size pieces.
2. Combine vinegar, sugar and mayonnaise. Chill in refrigerator.
3. When ready to serve, toss salad, onion, bacon, mandarin oranges and dressing.

Turkey & Grape Salad

This salad is made up of wonderful textures. Use it for lunch, along with a roll and some fruit.

¼ cup sour cream ✔
2 tablespoons plain rice vinegar
¼ cup mayonnaise
2 tablespoons sugar ✔
1 teaspoon kosher salt ✔
½ teaspoon pepper
1 lbs. turkey breasts, cut into ½ inch cubes ✔
2 cups seedless red grapes
1 cup walnuts ✔
8 oz. mozzarella cheese, cut into ½ inch cubes(optional)
4 stalks celery, diced
1 head romaine lettuce, chopped

1. In a medium bowl combine sour cream, vinegar, mayonnaise, sugar, salt and pepper. Set aside.
2. In a large bowl combine turkey, grapes, walnuts and cheese. Place in an airtight container. Pour the sour cream dressing over the turkey. Mix gently and seal container.
3. Place in refrigerator for at least 8 hours. When ready to serve, add diced celery and mix gently. Arrange the romaine lettuce on the bottom of a serving dish and place the salad on top for serving.

Sauces, Dressings

&

Seasonings

Apricot-Raisin Chutney

Chutney is a great way to add a sweet and sour flavor to a dish.

2 tablespoons extra-virgin olive oil ✔
½ cup finely chopped onion
1 lb. apricots, peeled, quartered and pitted
½ cup sugar ✔
½ cup good-quality honey
1/3 cup raisins
¼ cup apple cider vinegar

1. Heat the oil in a medium skillet over medium heat until hot, but not smoking. Add onion and cook until soft and translucent. About 4 minutes.
2. Transfer the onion to a large saucepan. Add the apricots, sugar, honey, raisins and vinegar. Cook over medium heat, stirring until thickened. About 25 minutes.
3. Pour chutney into a large bowl and allow to cool. The chutney can be refrigerated in an airtight container for up to 1 week. Bring to room temperature before serving.

Au Jus

2 tablespoons butter ✔
1 shallot, chopped
1 tablespoon flour ✔
4 cups beef broth ✔

In a large, shallow skillet over moderate heat, melt butter. Add shallots to butter and sauté 2 minutes. Add flour to shallots and cook a minute longer. Whisk in broth in a slow stream. Bring sauce to a boil and simmer over low heat until ready to serve.

BBQ Sauce

1 cup ketchup ✔
½ cup finely chopped onion
1/3 cup water
¼ cup butter ✔
1 tablespoon paprika
1 teaspoon brown sugar ✔
¼ teaspoon pepper
2 tablespoons lemon juice

Heat all ingredients except lemon juice in a sauce pan over medium heat. Bring to boil and add lemon juice.

Blue Cheese Dipping Sauce
Great with spicy buffalo wings and vegetables.

1 cup Greek yogurt ✓
¼ cup crumbled blue cheese
2 tablespoons finely grated red onion
2 tablespoons finely chopped fresh cilantro leaves
Salt ✓ and ground black pepper

Stir together the yogurt, blue cheese, red onion, cilantro and salt and pepper in a bowl. Refrigerate for at least 30 minutes before serving to allow the flavors to blend.

Brown Gravy

An old fashion recipe that is great with mashed potatoes.

2 tablespoons butter ✔
½ teaspoon sugar ✔
2 tablespoons flour ✔
1 cup beef broth ✔
Salt ✔ and pepper to taste

Melt butter in a saucepan over low heat. Add sugar and cook for 2 minutes. Stir occasionally. Add flour and cook for 3 minutes or until mixture has browned. Add broth and stir until smooth. Add salt and pepper to taste. Cook over low heat for 5 minutes. Stir frequently until thickened. Makes 1 cup.

(Easy) Caesar Dressing

2 garlic cloves
1 tablespoon Dijon mustard ✔
½ teaspoon salt ✔
¼ teaspoon pepper
¼ cup fresh lemon juice
½ cup extra-virgin olive oil ✔
½ cup Parmesan cheese ✔

1. Combine garlic, mustard, salt, pepper and lemon juice in a food processor and blend until smooth. With the food processor going, slowly add olive oil until blended. Add cheese and blend for 2 seconds.
2. Cover and chill for at least 2 hours before serving.

Caesar Dressing with Anchovies

4 garlic cloves
½ teaspoon salt ✔
12 anchovy fillets
1 tablespoon lemon zest
1 cup fresh lemon juice (about 3 lemons)
1 tablespoons drained capers, rinsed
1 ½ teaspoons dry mustard
½ teaspoon freshly ground pepper
1 cup extra-virgin olive oil ✔
½ cup finely grated Parmesan cheese ✔

1. Puree garlic, salt, anchovies, lemon zest, lemon juice, capers, mustard and pepper in a food processor. With machine running slowly add oil in a slow, steady stream, blending until emulsified.
2. Transfer to a medium bowl and stir in cheese.
3. The dressing can be refrigerated in an airtight container for up to 3 days. Bring to room temperature before serving.

Classic Cocktail Sauce

2 tablespoons grated peeled fresh horseradish
1 tablespoon fresh lemon juice
¼ teaspoon salt ✔
¾ cup ketchup ✔
¼ teaspoon hot sauce (optional)

Stir together the horseradish, lemon juice and salt in a small bowl. Stir in ketchup and hot sauce if desired. Cover and refrigerate until ready to serve.

Cocktail Sauce

A taste sensation without Worcestershire sauce.

1 cup mayonnaise
2 teaspoons hot chili sauce
1 teaspoon grated fresh ginger
½ teaspoon minced garlic
1 teaspoon minced green onions
1 teaspoon lime juice, or to taste
1 tablespoon freshly chopped cilantro leaves
½ teaspoon white pepper
¼ teaspoon salt ✔

Stir together the mayonnaise, hot chili sauce, ginger, garlic, green onions, lime juice, cilantro, white pepper and salt in a medium bowl and refrigerate, covered for half an hour before serving.

French Dressing

2 teaspoons tomato paste or ketchup ✔
1 ½ teaspoons sugar ✔
1 teaspoon finely grated onion
1 teaspoon dry mustard
¾ teaspoon paprika
¼ teaspoon salt ✔
¼ teaspoon celery seed
Dash of pepper
4 ½ teaspoons plain rice vinegar
1 ½ teaspoons lemon juice
½ cup oil ✔

Puree all ingredients except the oil in the bowl of a food processor. With the machine running, slowly add the oil in a slow, steady stream. Blend until emulsified.

Hawaiian Chutney

You can buy many types of chutney at the grocery store, but this one is so tasty and can accompany rice or meat dishes.

4 cups crushed, canned pineapple
2 cups chopped, seedless golden raisins
½ cup brown sugar, firmly packed ✔
3 tablespoons plain rice vinegar
1 teaspoon salt ✔
½ cup white sugar ✔
¼ teaspoon ground ginger
1/8 teaspoon cayenne pepper
¾ teaspoon ground allspice
¼ teaspoon ground cloves
¼ teaspoon ground cinnamon
A few drops of hot chili sauce
½ cup chopped almonds

1. Combine pineapple, raisins, brown sugar, vinegar and salt in large saucepan.
2. In a small bowl combine white sugar, ground ginger, cayenne pepper, ground allspice, ground cloves, ground cinnamon and chili sauce. Stir spice mixture into pineapple mixture; cook, stirring frequently over low heat for 40 minutes or until mixture becomes clear.
3. Remove from heat; add almonds.
4. Pour into hot, sterilize pint jars. Seal at once. Makes 3 pints.

Chutney may be stored in an airtight container in the refrigerator for up to 1 week, or processed as directed below and kept for up to 1 year.

1. Sterilize 3 pint-sized jars and their metal lids according to the manufacturer's instructions.
2. Spoon the hot mixture into the jars, filling to within 1/2-inch of the rim. With a clean, damp towel, wipe the rims and fit with a hot lid. Tightly screw on the metal ring.
3. Place jars, without touching, on a rack in a large, deep canning kettle or stockpot of rapidly boiling water; water should cover the cans by 1 inch. Boil and process for 15 minutes.
4. Using tongs, remove the jars, place on a towel and let cool completely before storing. Test the seals and tighten the rings as needed.
5. Store in a cool, dark place. After opening, store jars in the refrigerator.

Hollandaise Sauce

What is not to love about a basic hollandaise sauce? This is great for eggs benedict or pour over steamed asparagus.

3 egg yolks
1 tablespoon lemon juice
½ cup firm butter ✔

1. Stir egg yolks and lemon juice vigorously in a 1 ½ quart saucepan. Add ¼ cup of butter. Heat over very low heat, stirring constantly with a wire whisk until butter is melted. Add remaining butter and continue stirring until butter is melted and sauce is thickened.
2. Serve hot or at room temperature.

Italian Dressing

1 cup extra-virgin olive oil ✓
¼ cup plain rice vinegar
2 tablespoons finely chopped onion
1 teaspoon sugar ✓
1 teaspoon dry mustard
1 teaspoon dried basil
½ teaspoon salt ✓
½ teaspoon dried oregano leaves
¼ teaspoon pepper
2 cloves garlic, minced

Place all ingredients in a jar and close the lid. Shake before serving.

Mayonnaise I
Mixing by hand method.

1 egg yolk*
½ teaspoon fine salt ✔
½ teaspoon dry mustard
2 pinches sugar ✔
2 teaspoons fresh squeezed lemon juice
1 tablespoon plain rice vinegar
1 cup safflower oil ✔

In a glass bowl, whisk together egg yolk and dry ingredients. Combine lemon juice and vinegar in a separate bowl then thoroughly whisk half into the yolk mixture. Start whisking briskly, then start adding the oil a few drops at a time until the liquid seems to thicken and lighten a bit, (which means you've got an emulsion on your hands). Once you reach that point you can relax your arm a little (but just a little) and increase the oil flow to a constant thin stream. Once half of the oil is in add the rest of the lemon juice mixture. Continue whisking until all of the oil is incorporated. Leave at room temperature for 1 to 2 hours then refrigerate for up to 1 week.

*RAW EGG WARNING - *I suggest caution in consuming raw and lightly-cooked eggs due to the slight risk of Salmonella or other food-borne illness. To reduce this risk, I recommend you use only fresh, properly-refrigerated, clean, grade A or AA eggs with intact shells and avoid contact between the yolks or whites and the shell.*

Mayonnaise II
Food processor method.

2 tablespoons plain rice vinegar
2 tablespoons lime juice
1 egg yolk*
1 whole egg*
1 teaspoon fine grain salt ✓
1 teaspoon dry mustard
¼ teaspoon sugar ✓
2 cups safflower oil ✓

Add all ingredients except the oil to the bowl of a food processor. Pulse 5 times. Turn processor on and add oil in a steady stream until incorporated. Keep at room temperature for 2 hours. Refrigerate for up to 1 week.

*RAW EGG WARNING - *I suggest caution in consuming raw and lightly-cooked eggs due to the slight risk of Salmonella or other food-borne illness. To reduce this risk, I recommend you use only fresh, properly-refrigerated, clean, grade A or AA eggs with intact shells and avoid contact between the yolks or whites and the shell.*

Oriental Dressing

This is a fabulous sweet and sour dressing that can be served on a salad of shredded lettuce, chicken and toasted almonds.

¼ cup sugar ✓
1 teaspoon salt ✓
½ teaspoon pepper
6 tablespoons plain rice vinegar
½ cup sesame seed oil

Combine ingredients in a jar and shake to mix. Allow to set until the sugar dissolves.

Pan Gravy

¼ cup fat drippings from meat
¼ cup flour ✓
2 cups liquid (meat juices plus water or broth)
Salt ✓ and pepper

1. Remove meat from pan and keep warm. Pour meat juices into a large measuring cup. Skim off fat, reserving ¼ cup. Return reserved fat to pan and heat until bubbly. Stir in flour. Cook over low heat. Continuously stir until mixture is thickened.
2. Remove pan from heat. Add 2 cups liquid and stir. Return to heat and bring to a boil. Reduce heat and simmer for 4 minutes. Continuously stir until thickened. Add salt and pepper to taste. Makes 2 cups.

Pear Chutney

This chutney can be used with either meat or curry dishes. It is perfect for those who love pears.

¼ cup walnuts
1 teaspoon extra-virgin olive oil ✓
1 minced shallot
2 ripe, but firm pears, cored and diced
6 tablespoons apple cider vinegar
3 tablespoons good-quality honey
4 whole cloves
¼ cup golden raisins

1. Preheat oven to 375 degrees F. Spread walnuts on a small rimmed baking sheet and toast until lightly browned. About 7 to 9 minutes. Remove from oven and allow to cool. Chop walnuts and set aside.

2. Heat oil in a small saucepan over medium heat. Add shallot and sauté until softened. About 2 minutes. Add pears, vinegar, honey and cloves. Bring to a boil, reduce heat and simmer until pears are tender. About 5 minutes. Discard cloves. Stir in raisins and walnuts. Remove from heat. Serve warm or at room temperature.

Pesto Sauce

Use this sauce on any type of pasta. To save time make several batches and freeze for later.

2 ½ cups packed fresh basil leaves
1 garlic clove
4 anchovy fillets, rinsed
½ cup walnut halves, toasted
1 teaspoon lemon zest
¾ cup plus 2 tablespoons extra-virgin olive oil ✔
Salt ✔ and pepper

Combine basil, garlic, anchovies, walnuts and lemon zest in a food processor and blend until finely chopped. With machine running, add oil in a slow, steady stream until combined. Season with salt and pepper. Cover and store in refrigerator or freezer until ready to use. Makes 1 ¼ cups.

Ranch Dressing

Have you missed this old favorite? It's tasty and savory without the MSG.

1 chopped scallion
1 garlic clove
1 cup mayonnaise
1/3 cup buttermilk ✔
1 teaspoon plain rice vinegar
½ teaspoon kosher salt ✔
2 tablespoons fresh flat-leaf parsley
Dash of pepper

1. Place scallion and garlic in the bowl of a food processor and processor until garlic is minced. Add mayonnaise, buttermilk, vinegar and salt. Process until blended. Transfer into a bowl.
2. Chop parsley and stir into dressing. Add pepper to taste.

Russian Dressing

1 cup mayonnaise
¼ cup chili sauce
1 teaspoon finely chopped onion
½ teaspoon paprika

Mix all ingredients together. Place in an airtight container and refrigerate.

Sweet & Sour Sauce

This is great with eggs rolls to chicken nuggets and everything in between.

½ cup brown sugar ✔
2 tablespoon flour ✔
1/3 cup plain rice vinegar
1/3 cup pineapple juice
¼ cup finely chopped green pepper
2 tablespoons chopped pimiento
1 teaspoon salt ✔
¼ teaspoon garlic powder
¼ teaspoon ground ginger

1. In a small saucepan combine brown sugar and flour. Stir in vinegar, pineapple juice, green pepper, pimiento, salt, garlic powder and ginger. Cook and stir until thickened and bubbly. Cook and stir 2 minutes more.
2. Serve warm. Makes about 1 ¼ cups.

Taco Seasoning Mix

½ cup dried minced onions
5 tablespoons chili powder
3 tablespoons dried oregano
4 tablespoons flour (optional) ✔
2 tablespoons basil
2 tablespoons crushed red pepper flakes
2 tablespoons garlic powder

Combine all ingredients. Store in an airtight container.

Tartar Sauce

All I can say is what doesn't go with tartar sauce? From fish to chicken nuggets, but my favorite is still fries with a little ketchup mixed with the tartar sauce.

1 cup mayonnaise
1 tablespoon lemon juice
½ cup drained sweet pickle relish or 2 diced pickles ✔
1 tablespoon parsley
1 teaspoon grated onion
½ teaspoon salt ✔

Combine all ingredients and mix well. Cover and refrigerate for at least 2 hours before serving.

Thousand Island Dressing

This old-fashion favorite is always a staple in our house.

1 cup mayonnaise
1 tablespoon chopped fresh parsley
2 tablespoons diced dill pickles ✔
2 tablespoons ketchup ✔
1 teaspoon finely chopped onion
½ teaspoon paprika
1 hard cooked eggs, chopped

Mix all ingredients together. Place in an airtight container and refrigerate.

Soups

Baked Potato Soup

I often make this creamy soup for new mothers and their families. Kids love adding their own garnishes.

4 large potatoes
12 strips of bacon ✔
2/3 cup butter ✔
1 cup flour ✔
4 cups whipping cream ✔
3 cups milk ✔
4 diced green onions
1 ¼ cups white Cheddar cheese
1 cup sour cream ✔
¾ teaspoon salt ✔
½ teaspoon white pepper

1. Bake potatoes, cool, peel and cube.
2. Cook bacon, drain and crumble.
3. In a large soup pot melt butter over medium-low heat. Stir in flour. Stir until smooth and bubbly.
4. Gradually add whipping cream and milk. Stirring constantly until soup thickens.
5. Add potatoes and onions. Stir until it boils. Simmer gently for 10 minutes.
6. Add ½ of bacon, cheese, sour cream, salt and pepper. Stir until cheese is melted.
7. Garnish with bacon, green onion, cheese and sour cream.

Beef & Tomato Noodle Soup

3 medium chopped onions
3 tablespoons butter ✔
2 lbs. beef steak or stew meat cut into 1 inch cubes
2 teaspoons salt ✔
¼ teaspoon pepper
2 teaspoons paprika
2 6oz. cans tomato paste ✔
2 ½ cups beef broth ✔
4 cups water
2 medium diced green peppers
4 oz. noodles
3 garlic cloves, minced
½ teaspoon caraway seeds
¼ cup chopped parsley
¼ teaspoon marjoram

1. In a large saucepan sauté onions in butter until golden brown. Add beef, salt, pepper and paprika. Cover and cook over low heat for 15 minutes.
2. Add tomato paste, beef broth and water. Cover and cook until meat is nearly done, 1 ½ to 2 hours.
3. Add green peppers and cook uncovered for 20 minutes.
4. Meanwhile, cook noodles until tender. Drain noodles. Add noodles, garlic, caraway, parsley and marjoram to soup. Cook for 10 minutes.

Beef Barley Soup

This is one of the best soups I have ever made. It's a recipe from Jan, a friend of my mom. If you pick one of Jan's tasty recipes from our church and school cookbooks you can always count on it being delish.

1 lb. stew meat
2 teaspoons oil ✔
1 medium diced onion
½ cup beef broth ✔
6 cups water
1 cup barley
3 stalks celery, diced
2 potatoes, diced
5 carrots, sliced
1 10½ oz. can tomato soup

1. In a large soup pot brown stew meat and onion in oil.
2. Add beef broth and water and bring to a boil.
3. Add barley, celery, potato, carrots and tomato soup. Simmer for 1 hour or until barley is tender.

Chicken Noodle Soup

Nothing spells comfort more than the words chicken and noodles. You may replace the noodles with rice.

2 cups of cooked, cut up chicken ✔
3 sliced carrots
1 chopped small onion
2 chopped celery sticks
2 potatoes, pealed and cubed
4 cups chicken broth ✔
4 cups water
1 teaspoon parsley
1 teaspoon dill
1 bay leaf
1/8 teaspoon pepper
1 teaspoon salt ✔
2 cups noodles

1. Place all ingredients, except noodles, in a large soup pot. Bring to a boil and simmer for 40 minutes.
2. Add noodles and boil for 20 minutes.

Chicken Tortilla Soup

Both attractive and delicious, this soup is the full meal deal.

½ cup chopped onion
1 teaspoon minced garlic
2 tablespoons butter ✔
6 cups chicken broth ✔
1 cup salsa ✔
2 cups chopped cooked chicken ✔
½ cup chopped red pepper
¼ teaspoon pepper
2 bay leaves
6 - 6 inch corn tortillas, cut into ½ inch wide pieces ✔
½ cup oil ✔
2 avocados, peeled, cut into ½ inch wide pieces
1 cup shredded Cheddar cheese
¾ cup sour cream ✔

1. In a large soup pot sauté onion and garlic in butter over medium heat until onion is tender. Add broth, salsa, chicken, red pepper, pepper and bay leaves. Bring to a boil. Simmer and cover for 20 minutes. Stirring occasionally.
2. Discard bay leaves.
3. In a medium skillet fry the tortilla strips in oil over medium heat until light golden brown. Drain on a paper towel.
4. Place an equal amount of tortilla strips in 6 soup bowls. Ladle the soup over the strips.
5. Garnish with avocados, cheese and sour cream.

Corn Chowder

Only a few ingredients but a lot of flavor! You may replace the canned corn with fresh corn or even creamed corn.

5 slices bacon ✔
1 chopped medium onion
2 cups canned whole kernel corn
1 cup diced cooked potatoes
3 cups milk ✔
2 teaspoons salt ✔
¼ teaspoon white pepper
1 cup diced carrots

In a soup pot cook bacon until crisp. Remove bacon. Sauté onion in the bacon drippings until tender. Add remaining ingredients. Bring to a boil and simmer for 5 minutes.

Dutch Pea Soup

This recipe makes a huge pot of soup. Although good when first made, it is even better on the second day. I freeze the soup in containers holding 3 servings, to be defrosted and heated up when I'm pressed for time.

1 lb. dried peas
1 medium ham hock ✓
2 quarts water
2 teaspoons salt ✓
½ teaspoon pepper
1 ½ cups chopped celery
2 chopped onions
3 chopped potatoes
2 chopped carrots
1 teaspoon parsley
1 cup milk ✓

1. Sort and rinse peas. Soak peas in cold water for 12 hours.
2. Cook ham hock, peas and water in a saucepan over medium heat for 2 hours. Remove ham hock and take off meat. Cut into bite-size pieces and return to pan.
3. Add salt, pepper, celery, onions, potatoes and carrots. Mix gently. Cook for 1 hour.
4. Add parsley and milk. Cook over low heat for 10 minutes.

Egg Drop Soup

When asked what I missed on a MSG free diet, I admitted that it was Chinese Food. I have a hard time resisting those sweet and salty flavors. Now I don't have to miss them anymore.

3 cups chicken broth ✔
2 eggs, beaten
1/3 cup chopped green onions
¾ cup diced carrots
¼ cup chopped water chestnuts
½ teaspoon salt ✔
¼ cup frozen peas

1. In a large saucepan bring broth to a boil. Gradually add the egg, stirring briskly after each addition.
2. Add onions, carrots, chestnuts and salt. Simmer until carrots are tender-crisp.
3. Add peas and simmer for 5 minutes.

New England Clam Chowder

Finally a clam chowder without MSG or should I say, "secret herbs and spices."

1 pint shucked clams or 2 6½oz. cans minced clams
2 slices of bacon ✔
2 ½ cups finely chopped, peeled potatoes
1 cup chopped onion
1 teaspoon salt ✔
¼ teaspoon dried thyme
¼ teaspoon pepper
2 cups milk ✔
1 cup cream ✔
2 tablespoons flour ✔

1. Chop shucked clams, reserving juice. Set clams aside. Strain clam juice to remove bits of shell. If necessary, add water to clam juice to equal 1 cup. Set aside.
2. In a large saucepan cook bacon until crisp. Remove bacon, reserving 1 tablespoon of drippings. Drain bacon on paper towels, crumble and set aside.
3. In the same saucepan combine reserved bacon drippings, reserved clam juice, potatoes, onion, salt, thyme and pepper. Bring to a boil on medium heat. Reduce heat and simmer for 10 minutes or until potatoes are tender. With the back of a fork, mash potatoes slightly against the side of the pan.
4. In a small bowl combine milk, cream and flour until smooth. Add to potato mixture. Cook and stir until slightly thickened and bubbly. Stir in clams. Return to boiling. Reduce heat and cook for 2 minutes.
5. Serve in bowls and garnish with bacon.

Taco Soup

I often make this hearty soup a day ahead and put it in a crock pot for those busy days when I don't have time to make dinner.

1 lb. ground beef
3 tablespoons taco seasoning ✔
½ cup water
1 16oz. can whole kernel corn
1 15oz. can tomato sauce ✔
1 15oz. can stewed tomatoes
1 15oz. can kidney beans
1 jar salsa ✔
2 cups shredded cheese
4 cups corn chips ✔
1 pint sour cream ✔

1. Brown beef in a large sauce pan over medium heat. Mix taco seasoning and water together. Add to beef. Simmer for 5 minutes. Add corn, tomato sauce, tomatoes, beans and salsa. Simmer for 1 hour or on low in a crock pot for 4 hours.
2. Serve with shredded cheese, chips and sour cream.

Index

CPSIA information can be obtained at www.ICGtesting.com
Printed in the USA
BVOW02s1148050116

431641BV00004B/165/P

9 780615 257570